THE GITA FOR KIDS

The Enchanted Odyssey

Table Of Contents

VOCABULARY

Chariot-small carriage pulled by horses

Valiant-fearless

Trembling-shaking

Colossal-huge

Distraught-very worried

Dilemma-difficult or puzzled situation

Righteousness- being morally right/justified

Profound-very great

Indestructible-cannot be easily damaged or destroyed

Pervade-spread through all parts

Interconnectedness-the state of being connected with each other

Compassion-understanding for somebody

who is suffering

Possessions-something that you own

Transitory-existing only for a short time

Perceive- notice something

Impermanence the state or fact of lasting for only a limited period of time

Liberation-the act of freeing something

Implications-indirect future results of some actions

Impending- likely to occur soon/upcoming

Renounce- refusing with formal declaration

Equanimity- a calm state of mind

Contrary- opposite

Integrity-the quality of being honest

Harmonious- peaceful and without disagreement

Lineage-a group of individuals from a common ancestor

Contemplation-an act of considering with

attention

Discernment- the ability to judge well

Perishable- likely to die or decay

Equanimity- a calm state of mind

Confined-very small

Diligently-uses a lot of effort

Integrating-blend into a functioning

Embark- to begin (a journey)

Insatiable-very great

Renunciation- sacrificing something

Tranquil- quiet and peaceful

Attune- make receptive or aware

Elucidates-explain something

Profound-Very Great

Indestructible-Cannot Be Easily Damaged Or Destroyed

Pervade-Spread Through All Parts

Interconnectedness-The State Of Being

Connected With Each Other

Compassion-Understanding For Somebody Who Is Suffering

Possessions-Something That You Own

Transitory-Existing Only For A Short Time

Implications-Indirect Future Results Of Some Actions

Impending- Likely To Occur Soon/Upcoming

Renounce- Refusing With Formal Declaration

Embrace-To Hold Something

Equanimity- A Calm State Of Mind

Contrary- Opposite

Integrity-The Quality Of Being Honest

Harmonious- Peaceful And Without Disagreement

Lineage-A Group Of Individuals From A Common Ancestor

Contemplation-An Act Of Considering With

Attention

Discernment- The Ability To Judge Well

Perishable- Likely To Die Or Decay

Equanimity- A Calm State Of Mind

Confined-Very Small

Renunciation- Sacrificing Something

Tranquil- Quiet And Peaceful

Attune- Make Receptive Or Aware

Elucidates-Explain Something

Tranquil- Quiet And Peaceful

Turbulent-Moving In A Violent Way

Perseverance- Not Giving Up/ The Effort Required To Do Something

Steadfast Faithful And Loyal

Fostering-Encourage The Development Of Something

Compassionate-Feeling Or Showing Empathy

Deceitfulness-Hiding Truth

Succumbing-To Stop Fighting Against Something

Bondage-The State Of Being A Slave

Embodying To Be An Example Of Or Expres

ACKNOWLEDGEMENT

I would like to thank and express gratitude to all those who encouraged me to write and supported me in this beautiful journey of understanding Gita.

My parents who were my go to fact checker at every step, my husband for the immense encouragement, my sister and brother who have been the best critic and gave the most honest feedbacks, my nieces who were my very first readers of the age group, giving me valuable insight from their understanding.

My friends, for their love and support throughout the journey.

Finally, I would like to thank you, the reader, for picking up this book. I hope you enjoy the journey yourself and your loved little one.

DEDICATION

Dedicated to my Grandfather Mr. S.K. Mishra

DISCLAIMER

This novel is inspired from Bhagvada Gita.

The author of this novel does not claim to be an expert on the Gita.

The Gita is a complex and ancient text with many different interpretations. This novel is one interpretation of the same, and it is not meant to be the definitive version of the story.

The author has taken some liberties with the Gita in order to create a more engaging and educative experience for the children and their parents.

CHAPTER 1: THE PRINCE AND THE CHARIOTEER

Once upon a time, in the ancient kingdom of Kurukshetra, there lived a young prince named Arjuna. He was a skilled warrior and archer, known for his bravery and valiant deeds. Arjuna was part of a great royal family, and his kingdom was about to face a momentous event—a colossal war between two groups of cousins, known as the Pandavas and the Kauravas.

As the war was about to begin, Arjuna found himself standing on the battlefield, surrounded by his fellow warriors, friends, and family members. But instead of being ready for battle, he was overwhelmed with a mix of confusion, sadness, and doubt. He gazed across the field and saw his own relatives and dear friends among the opposing forces. The thought of fighting and causing harm to his loved ones made his heart heavy with sorrow.

*The armies of Pandavas and Kauravas
stand face to face ready to fight*

"My whole body is trembling, my hair is standing on end, my bow Gandiva is slipping from my hand, and my skin is burning."

Feeling distraught, Arjuna turned to his

charioteer, Krishna, for guidance. Krishna, who was not just an ordinary charioteer but an incarnation of the divine, listened attentively to Arjuna's concerns. He could sense the turmoil within the prince's heart and understood the depth of his dilemma.

Krishna began to enlighten Arjuna, teaching him about life, duty, and the path to righteousness. He spoke gently and compassionately, reassuring Arjuna that his doubts and confusion were not uncommon. Krishna explained that it was natural for a noble soul like Arjuna to experience such emotions when faced with the prospect of causing harm to others, especially those he loved.

Krishna emphasized that life is full of challenges, and every person has their own unique set of responsibilities and duties. He reminded Arjuna of his role as a prince, a warrior, and a protector of righteousness. He spoke of the importance of fulfilling one's duty with dedication and selflessness, even in the face of difficult choices.

Krishna taught Arjuna that attachment to the physical body and the temporary relationships of this world leads to suffering. He explained the concept of the eternal soul, which is indestructible and transcends life and death.

Krishna assured Arjuna that the soul is eternal and that the physical body is just a temporary vessel.

Arjun, deep in his thoughts feeling distraught and anxious

"For the soul there is neither birth nor death at any time. He/She has not come into being, does not come into being, and will not come into being. He/She is unborn, eternal, ever existing and primeval. He/She is not slain when the body is slain."

Furthermore, Krishna stressed the significance of detachment from the outcomes of one's actions. He encouraged Arjuna to focus on performing his duty selflessly, without seeking personal gains or becoming attached to the results. Krishna explained that by surrendering the fruits of his actions to the divine, Arjuna could find peace and overcome the moral dilemmas he faced.

As Krishna shared his wisdom, Arjuna's confusion began to dissipate. He started to understand that he had a responsibility to uphold righteousness and protect the innocent, even if it meant engaging in the battle. Arjuna realized that his attachment to his loved ones was clouding his judgment, and by aligning himself with the greater good, he could transcend his personal desires.

Filled with newfound clarity and determination, Arjuna expressed his gratitude to Krishna for guiding him through his inner turmoil. He prepared himself to fulfill his duty as a warrior, understanding that the war was not just a physical battle, but also a spiritual journey of self-realization and righteousness.

The first chapter of the Bhagavad Gita, "The Prince and the Charioteer," sets the stage for the profound teachings that Krishna imparts to Arjuna. It introduces the moral and ethical conflicts that Arjuna faces, his doubts and dilemmas, and Krishna's role as his divine guide and mentor. This chapter lays the foundation for the subsequent teachings, which delve deeper into the nature of the self, the paths to enlightenment, and the principles of righteous living.

❖ ❖ ❖

There were once two best friends, Ani and Noa. They were inseparable. They studied, played and even lived across the street from each other. Their bus rides to school would be a riot and even in class they were a team that worked and sparkled together.

One day in class, the class teacher, Miss Mehta brought a bag of candies and passed across the class. The exercise was that each child had to pick only one candy from the big bag. Even if you loved it a lot, you were not allowed to pick more than one. The bag circulated and it eventually reached the bench of Ani and Noa. Ani picked one candy and passed the bag to Noa. Noa was too fond of candies and could not resist. She picked an extra candy and gestured Ani to keep quiet. Being the best friend that Ani was, she did not speak.

Ani and Noa along with their classmates in school

The class was over and they went home. Ani was restless that night and didn't even have her dinner properly. Her mom realised something is amiss. She went in her room and asked her to discuss anything if it was bothering her. Ani divided with the dilemma shared the entire incident with her mother. Her mother then explained her the meaning of true friendship. "If you really care about your friend, you will make sure you show her the right path no matter how hard it is for you. Do not feel that you are betraying her just because you are choosing the right thing to do."

Ani and her mother reading a bedtime story

Next day at school when the exercise was being

concluded by the teacher, Ani encouraged and counselled Noa to tell the truth. Noa understood and did the same. The teacher was overwhelmed by the gesture and explained the class the importance of honesty and true friendship.

This story tells us that sharing the dilemma with our loved and trusted ones will always give us the right path. It also tells us that there are hard times when it is difficult choose relationships over ethics. It is at this time that we seek the guidance of our parents and elders for choosing the right path. Very similar to the incident that we have read before between Krishna and Arjun. When in dilemma, turn to the person you trust and respect and you shall always find the correct path.

CHAPTER 2: THE ETERNAL SOUL

Krishna imparts profound wisdom to Arjuna, unveiling the nature of the self and the eternal soul that resides within each living being.

Krishna begins by explaining that life is like a journey, and our physical bodies are merely temporary vessels for the eternal soul. He emphasizes that the soul is immortal, indestructible, and beyond the realms of birth and death. The soul is a fragment of the divine energy that pervades the entire universe, connecting all living beings.

Krishna assures Arjuna that even if his body perishes in the battle, his soul will continue its eternal journey. This understanding serves to alleviate Arjuna's fear of death and helps him realize that his true identity lies not in the perishable body but in the immortal soul.

Furthermore, Krishna elucidates the concept of the interconnectedness of all souls. He explains that every being in existence is a manifestation of the divine and that the same eternal soul resides within all living entities. This understanding promotes unity, compassion, and respect for all life forms.

Krishna stresses the importance of fulfilling one's duties and responsibilities in accordance with one's nature and position in society. He reminds Arjuna that as a warrior and prince, it is his duty to protect righteousness, uphold justice, and maintain social order. However, Krishna emphasizes that Arjuna should perform his duties without attachment to the outcomes, recognizing that the soul is unaffected by success or failure.

"Perform your prescribed duties, for doing so is better than not working. One cannot even maintain one's physical body without work"

Krishna's teachings emphasize the need to rise above worldly attachments and desires that bind individuals to the cycle of birth and death. He explains that the pursuit of material possessions and sensory pleasures can lead to suffering and transitory happiness. Instead, Krishna encourages Arjuna to focus on attaining spiritual enlightenment, which brings everlasting peace and fulfillment.

By understanding the eternal nature of the soul, Krishna teaches Arjuna to perceive life from a broader perspective. He encourages Arjuna to embrace his divine nature and recognize the inherent divinity in all beings. This understanding allows one to transcend the ego and act with love, compassion, and selflessness.

Arjun perplexed awaits Shri Krishna

The teachings in this chapter invite individuals to reflect upon their own existence and recognize the impermanence of the physical body. By realizing the eternal nature of the soul and cultivating a sense of interconnectedness, individuals can lead a life rooted in spiritual values, inner peace, and harmony with the universe.

"The Eternal Soul" chapter in the Bhagavad Gita serves as a profound reminder of the true essence of life and the eternal nature of the soul. It offers guidance on how to navigate the transient nature of the physical world and strive towards self-realization, liberation, and spiritual growth.

◆ ◆ ◆

Title: The Little Whisperer

Once upon a time, in a colorful land filled with talking animals and magical creatures, there lived a young fox named Maddy. Maddy was a curious and adventurous little fox, always exploring the forest and seeking new experiences. However, he often found himself getting into trouble because he didn't listen to his inner voice.

One sunny morning, as Maddy was exploring the

deep woods, he stumbled upon a mysterious cave. The cave seemed to whisper a soft, gentle voice, warning him to be cautious. But Maddy was too excited to explore something new and decided to enter the cave, ignoring the whisper of his inner voice.

Maddy excited to enter the mysterious cave

Inside the cave, he discovered glittering gems and sparkling crystals. The sight was breathtaking, and for a moment, Maddy forgot about everything *else. However, as he reached out to touch the precious stones, the cave suddenly trembled, and a huge boulder blocked the entrance, trapping Maddy inside!*

Maddy felt scared and alone in the dark cave, and he wished he had listened to his inner voice, which had warned him to be cautious. Now, he realized that he needed to pay more attention to his instincts and the little voice inside him.

Back in the outside world, Maddy's friends and family grew worried when he didn't return. They decided to search for him throughout the forest. Among them was an old owl named Oliver, known for his wisdom and the ability to listen to his inner voice.

Oliver knew that the key to finding Maddy lay in listening carefully to his heart. So, as he searched, he closed his eyes and focused on his inner voice, guiding him in the right direction.

Meanwhile, inside the cave, Maddy began to feel hopeless. Just when he was about to give up, he remembered something his parents had told him about finding strength in silence and listening to his inner voice. He closed his eyes and tried to listen to what his heart was telling him.

And there it was, a soft whisper, almost like a gentle

breeze, guiding him to look up. To his surprise, he saw a tiny opening in the cave's roof, just big enough for him to crawl through. Eagerly, Maddy climbed up and squeezed out, finally free from the dark cave.

As he emerged into the sunlight, Maddy saw his friends and family waiting for him. They all hugged him tightly, relieved to have him back safe and sound. Maddy felt grateful for their love and support but knew that he should have listened to his inner voice from the start.

From that day forward, Maddy promised himself that he would always pay attention to his inner voice. He learned that it was like having a wise friend inside him, guiding him through difficult situations and helping him make the right choices.

And so, the little fox named Maddy grew wiser and happier, thanks to the valuable lesson he learned about the importance of his inner voice. And whenever he faced a tough decision or felt unsure about something, he would close his eyes, listen carefully, and let the gentle whisper inside guide him.

CHAPTER 3: SELFLESS ACTION

Krishna imparts teachings to Arjuna about the significance of performing one's duties selflessly and without attachment to the results. This chapter delves into the concept of karma yoga, the path of selfless action.

Krishna begins by addressing Arjuna's concerns about the moral implications of engaging in the impending battle. Arjuna wonders if it would be better to renounce the battle altogether and withdraw from his responsibilities as a warrior. However, Krishna emphasizes the importance of fulfilling one's duty according to one's nature and social position.

Krishna explains that every individual is bound by their inherent nature and qualities (guna) and their respective duties (swadharma) in society. He asserts that it is through the performance of these duties that one can contribute to the well-being of the world. Krishna advises Arjuna to embrace his duty as a warrior, fight for righteousness, and fulfill his responsibilities without hesitation.

Furthermore, Krishna introduces the concept of selfless action, emphasizing that the focus should be on the action itself rather than the outcome. He encourages Arjuna to detach himself from the desire for personal gain or success and instead perform his actions as an offering to the divine.

Krishna explains that the results of actions are not within our control, as they are influenced by numerous factors beyond our grasp. Therefore, it is essential to surrender the fruits of our actions to the divine and not be swayed by success or failure. By doing so, one can cultivate a sense of equanimity and inner peace.

Krishna reminds Arjuna that even he, as the divine charioteer, engages in action without attachment. Despite being the supreme lord, Krishna carries out his duties in the world without personal desire or ego. He serves as an example of selfless action and encourages Arjuna to follow suit.

Through selfless action, Krishna explains, one can transcend the cycle of karma and attain spiritual growth. By performing actions without selfish motives, one purifies the mind, develops self-discipline, and ultimately realizes the divinity within.

Krishna emphasizes that non-action is not a solution to Arjuna's dilemma. Renouncing action altogether would be contrary to his duty and lead to negative consequences. Instead, Krishna urges Arjuna to engage in action with a selfless and dedicated mindset, understanding that action is an essential aspect of life.

This chapter serves as a reminder that action is an integral part of the human experience, and it is through selfless action that individuals can find meaning, fulfillment, and spiritual progress. It teaches the importance of performing duties with dedication, integrity, and a sense of service to the greater good.

By embracing the path of selfless action, individuals can cultivate a harmonious relationship with the world, contribute positively to society, and attain a higher level of consciousness. The teachings in this chapter encourage individuals to align their actions with divine principles, transcending personal desires and contributing to the welfare of all beings.

◆ ◆ ◆

Once upon a time, in a lively village surrounded by rolling hills and colorful gardens, there lived a young elephant named Nimmi. Nimmi had a big heart and always looked for ways to help others. She believed that small acts of kindness could make a big difference in the world.

One sunny morning, as Nimmi strolled through the village, she noticed a group of animals gathered around a tree. They were all chirping, tweeting, and squeaking with concern. Nimmi approached and discovered a family of birds frantically trying to build a nest, but they were struggling to find suitable twigs and leaves.

Nimmi's compassionate nature kicked in, and she knew she could assist them. With her strong trunk and gentle touch, she carefully plucked the finest twigs and leaves from the surrounding trees, providing the birds with perfect building materials.

Nimmi being loved and admired by all other animals

As Nimmi helped the birds, the animals around her watched in awe. They admired her selfless actions and were inspired by her kindness. Word quickly spread throughout the village about Nimmi's helpful nature.

The following day, as Nimmi ventured through the village again, she noticed a line of animals waiting outside a small bakery. The bakery was known for its mouthwatering treats, but today there was *a problem—the bakery's delivery cart had broken down, and they couldn't get fresh ingredients for their creations.*

Nimmi saw the disappointment on their faces and immediately knew what to do. She offered her assistance and decided to use her strength to pull the cart to the nearby fields where fresh ingredients awaited. With the animals cheering her on, Nimmi pulled the cart effortlessly, ensuring that everyone in the village could enjoy the bakery's delicious treats.

Nimmi's selfless actions didn't stop there. As time went on, she continued to lend a helping trunk to anyone in need. She carried heavy baskets for the tired rabbits, fetched water for the thirsty squirrels, and even helped the butterflies cross wide rivers.

The more Nimmi gave, the more joy she felt within her heart. She realized that selfless actions not only brought happiness to others but also filled her own life with a sense of purpose and fulfillment.

One day, as Nimmi did not feel well and rested under the shade of a giant tree, all the animals she had helped gathered around her. They wanted to express their gratitude for her selfless acts. Each animal shared a heartfelt story of how Nimmi's kindness had made a positive impact on their lives. They also offered her food.

Nimmi pulling the delivery cart of the bakery

Touched by their words and kind action, Nimmi shed tears of joy. She realized that her selfless actions had created a ripple effect of kindness, spreading love and compassion throughout the village.

From that day forward, Nimmi's selfless nature inspired others to follow in her footsteps. The village became a place where everyone looked out for one another, performing acts of kindness without hesitation. The spirit of selflessness bloomed like the most vibrant flower, making the village a joyful and harmonious place to live.

And so, the story of Nimmi the elephant teaches us the power of selfless actions. It reminds us that by caring for others and lending a helping hand, we can create a world filled with love, compassion, and unity. No act of kindness is too small, for even the smallest gesture can bring immense joy and make a remarkable difference in the lives of others.

Very similar to Krishna teaching Arjun about the selfless deeds that Arjun should perform without thinking of the rewards. Actions that are done without the greed of rewards are truly called as selfless. These deeds make us a better human.

CHAPTER 4: THE PATH OF KNOWLEDGE

In the Bhagavad Gita's fourth chapter, titled "The Path of Knowledge," Krishna imparts profound teachings to Arjuna about the importance of acquiring spiritual knowledge and the eternal nature of divine wisdom.

Krishna begins by revealing that he has taught this sacred knowledge to great sages and enlightened beings throughout history. He explains that he takes birth in various forms to restore righteousness, guide humanity, and uplift spiritual consciousness.

Krishna emphasizes that spiritual knowledge is eternal and has been passed down from generation to generation through a lineage of enlightened masters. He enlightens Arjuna about the importance of receiving knowledge from a realized teacher, highlighting the significance of a guru-disciple relationship.

Krishna introduces the concept of jnana

yoga, the path of knowledge, which involves acquiring self-realization through contemplation, discernment, and spiritual wisdom. He emphasizes that true knowledge is not mere intellectual understanding but the direct experience and realization of one's eternal essence.

Sages meditating for enlightenment. Sit down with your legs crossed and eyes closed

Krishna explains that the physical body is perishable, but the soul is eternal and transcendent. By understanding the eternal nature of the soul, one can develop a detached perspective towards the temporary nature of the physical world. This understanding enables individuals to navigate life's challenges with equanimity and embrace their higher spiritual purpose.

Krishna teaches that the realization of one's divine nature is not confined to any specific caste, gender, or social position. He emphasizes that anyone, regardless of their external circumstances, can attain spiritual enlightenment through devotion, self-discipline, and seeking the truth within.

Furthermore, Krishna reveals the principle of karma and its relationship with spiritual evolution. He explains that all actions leave imprints, or impressions (samskaras), on the mind, which influence one's future experiences and tendencies. By performing actions with selflessness, purity, and dedication, individuals can purify their minds and gradually transcend the cycle of karma.

"One who neither hates nor desires the fruits of their activities is known to be always renounced."

Krishna encourages Arjuna to embrace the path of knowledge and strive for self-realization. He assures him that by seeking the truth within and diligently practicing spiritual disciplines, one can overcome ignorance and experience the divine presence.

This chapter serves as a reminder of the significance of spiritual knowledge in guiding individuals towards self-realization and union with the divine. It highlights the importance of seeking a realized teacher, contemplating on eternal truths, and integrating spiritual wisdom into daily life.

By following the path of knowledge, individuals can cultivate discernment, expand their consciousness, and realize their oneness with the universal consciousness. The teachings in this chapter inspire individuals to embark on a journey of self-discovery, seeking wisdom that leads to liberation and inner fulfillment.

Once upon a time in a quiet village nestled amidst

rolling hills, there lived a young rabbit named Oliver. Oliver had an insatiable thirst for knowledge and a love for learning. He was always seen with a book in his paws, exploring the world through words and stories.

One sunny morning, as Oliver hopped through the village, he noticed an old and wise owl named Maya perched on a branch. Maya was known for her vast wisdom and knowledge of the world. Intrigued, Oliver approached her and asked, "Oh wise Maya, how can I walk the path of knowledge and discover the wonders of the world?"

Maya blinked her wise eyes and smiled warmly at Oliver. "Ah, young seeker of knowledge, your quest is noble. The path of knowledge begins with curiosity and a thirst for understanding. Ask questions, observe the world around you, and never stop seeking answers."

Curious Oliver chats with Maya, the owl

Oliver listened intently as Maya shared her wisdom. "First, my dear Oliver, explore the world with an open mind. Venture beyond the boundaries of your familiar surroundings. Discover new places, meet different creatures, and embrace diverse perspectives. Each encounter will teach you something new."

Excitement filled Oliver's heart as he imagined the adventures that lay ahead. He thanked Maya for her *guidance and set off on his journey to discover the wonders of the world.*

With each step, Oliver encountered various animals, each with their own unique knowledge and skills. He listened attentively as the ants taught him about cooperation and hard work. The bees shared their wisdom of harmony and the importance of pollination. The squirrels taught him the art of preparation and conservation.

Oliver's hunger for knowledge grew with each encounter. He soaked up every lesson, storing them like treasures in his mind. His collection of knowledge expanded, painting a vivid picture of the world's wonders.

But as Oliver continued his journey, he faced challenges and obstacles that tested his determination. He encountered riddles he couldn't solve and puzzles he couldn't crack. Doubt started to cloud his mind, and he questioned whether he had what it took to walk the path of knowledge.

One day, while resting near a babbling brook, Oliver met a wise tortoise named Theodore. Theodore had a shell covered in intricate patterns and a calming presence that instantly put Oliver at ease. Sensing his doubts, Theodore approached Oliver with a gentle smile.

"Dear Oliver," Theodore began, "the path of knowledge is not always smooth. It is filled with challenges and moments of uncertainty. But remember, true wisdom lies not only in knowing the answers but also in embracing the journey of seeking them."

Oliver pondered Theodore's words and found solace in them. He realized that the joy of knowledge came not just from finding answers but from the process of exploration, growth, and self-discovery.

With renewed determination, Oliver continued on his path. He explored ancient libraries, delved into scientific experiments, and sought wisdom from scholars and sages. Along the way, he discovered that knowledge was vast and ever-expanding, and he was merely a small part of its endless tapestry.

As years passed, Oliver became a wise and knowledgeable rabbit, revered by all in the village. He shared his wisdom with younger rabbits, encouraging them to embrace the path of knowledge with open hearts and curious minds.

And so, the story of Oliver the rabbit teaches us that the path of knowledge is a lifelong journey filled with curiosity, exploration, and the courage to ask questions. It reminds us that true wisdom lies not only in finding answers but in the pursuit of knowledge itself. By walking the path of knowledge, we unlock the secrets of the world and grow into wiser, more enlightened beings.

The essence of the story also reflects the ambiguities Arjun is facing. There will always be many people to guide you throughout your life, but living that life and experiencing the highs and lows is your job. Owning upto the mistakes that you made and accepting the challenges is your work. Only and only then can we actually follow the path of knowledge and be wise from our experiences.

CHAPTER 5: THE YOGA OF RENUNCIATION

Krishna imparts profound teachings to Arjuna about the path of renunciation and the importance of detaching oneself from worldly attachments.

Krishna begins by emphasizing the significance of both renunciation and selfless action in spiritual growth. He explains that renunciation does not imply abandoning all responsibilities and worldly duties but rather cultivating a mindset of detachment and offering one's actions to the divine.

Krishna introduces the concept of sannyasa, the path of renunciation, which involves letting go of attachments to the results of actions. He explains that when one performs actions without seeking personal gains, the mind becomes tranquil and attuned to the divine presence.

Ever tried sharing the most precious toy you have? What if your friend asks to take it home? Will you be okay with it?

Krishna further elucidates that true renunciation is not about physically renouncing possessions or relationships but rather renouncing the egoistic attachment to them. He emphasizes that true renunciation lies in performing one's duties with a sense of selflessness, without being swayed by desires or the fruits of actions.

Krishna describes the two paths of renunciation: the path of knowledge and the path of action. He explains that for those inclined towards contemplation and introspection, the path of knowledge is suitable. This path involves acquiring spiritual wisdom, discerning the eternal from the transient, and realizing one's true nature as the immortal soul.

Steps of Suryanamaskar. Can you do it?

For those inclined towards action and service, Krishna recommends the path of selfless action. He explains that by offering all actions to the divine and performing them without selfish motives, individuals can purify their minds and progress spiritually.

Krishna teaches that the mind is the key to spiritual progress. By mastering the mind and transcending its fluctuations, one can attain inner peace and liberation. He explains that a disciplined mind, free from distractions and desires, is essential for attaining self-realization.

Shri Krishna showing Arjun the right path

Furthermore, Krishna emphasizes the importance of controlling the senses and withdrawing from external distractions. By practicing sensory restraint and focusing the mind inward, individuals can develop a deep sense of inner calm and concentration.

Krishna also addresses the concept of equanimity, emphasizing the need to remain balanced in the face of pleasure and pain, success and failure. He teaches that true spiritual growth lies in maintaining an equanimous mind, unaffected by external circumstances.

Through the teachings in this chapter, Krishna highlights the importance of renunciation as a means to attain spiritual liberation. He encourages Arjuna to cultivate detachment and offer all actions to the divine, recognizing that true fulfillment lies in realizing the eternal nature of the soul.

"The Yoga of Renunciation" chapter serves as a guide for individuals seeking spiritual growth and liberation. It offers insights into the paths of knowledge and action, teaching the importance of renunciation, selflessness, and mastery of the mind. By practicing renunciation in daily life and aligning actions with divine principles, individuals can experience inner peace, spiritual evolution, and union with the divine.

Title: The Magic of Giving

In a faraway kingdom, nestled amidst rolling hills and blooming meadows, there lived a young girl named Lily. She was a kind and caring soul, always looking for ways to help others. One day, while taking a stroll through the village, she noticed a group of poor children playing with old, tattered toys.

Lily's heart filled with empathy, and she knew she had to do something to bring a smile to their faces. She decided to organize a charity fair to collect toys, clothes, and books for the less fortunate children in the village. Lily believed that together, they could spread happiness and share the magic of giving.

With the help of her friends and the villagers, Lily set up colorful stalls in the village square. The aroma of freshly baked cookies and the sound of cheerful laughter filled the air. Everyone was eager to contribute to the charity fair. They donated toys they had outgrown, clothes that were too small, and books they had already read.

As the fair began, children and adults alike were excited to see the array of treasures laid out on the stalls. They came together, buying items and leaving generous donations. All the while, Lily and her friends explained to everyone how their contributions would help the less fortunate children in the village.

Lily sets up a colourful stall for the villagers

One by one, the children from the poor neighborhood arrived at the fair. Their eyes sparkled with amazement as they received toys, clothes, and books they had never dreamed of having. Their joy knew no bounds, and they thanked Lily and her friends with big, warm smiles.

But the magic of giving did not end there. Lily had an idea to make the charity fair even more special. She proposed that a part of the donations should be used to plant fruit trees and create a community garden. This way, they could provide fresh fruits and vegetables for those in need throughout the year.

As the months passed, the village blossomed with kindness and generosity. The community garden thrived, and the joy of giving continued to spread. Lily's charity fair became an annual tradition, and more and more people joined in to support the cause.

One evening, a little girl named Mia approached Lily. She was holding a bag filled with her favorite toys. "Lily," Mia said, "I want to donate these toys to the charity fair. I realized that the joy of giving is even more magical than the joy of receiving."

Lily smiled warmly at Mia and hugged her tightly. "You are absolutely right, Mia," she said. "The magic of giving comes from the heart. And when we give selflessly, we create a world full of love and happiness for everyone."

And so, the village of Lily and her friends became a place where kindness and charity flourished. They learned that even the smallest act of giving could make a significant difference in someone's life. And as they continued to share the magic of giving, their hearts grew even brighter, making the world around them a little more beautiful every day.

CHAPTER 6: THE YOGA OF MEDITATION

Krishna imparts profound teachings to Arjuna about the practice of meditation and its role in attaining spiritual enlightenment.

Krishna begins by explaining the importance of solitude and finding a serene place for meditation. He emphasizes that a tranquil environment supports the practice of meditation, allowing individuals to turn their attention inward and connect with their higher selves.

Krishna introduces the concept of yoga as the union of the individual consciousness with the universal consciousness. He teaches Arjuna the practice of dhyana yoga, the yoga of meditation, as a means to attain this union. Through meditation, one can still the mind, transcend the limitations of the ego, and experience the divinity within.

Krishna describes the ideal posture for meditation, encouraging individuals to sit in a comfortable and steady position, with the spine erect and the body relaxed. He emphasizes the need for physical stillness to facilitate mental concentration and inner awareness.

Furthermore, Krishna explains that the mind is restless and challenging to control. He compares it to a turbulent wind that constantly fluctuates. However, with practice and detachment, individuals can train the mind to be calm and focused. Krishna teaches Arjuna the importance of discipline and perseverance in mastering the mind.

Krishna also highlights the role of detachment in meditation. He advises Arjuna to detach himself from sensory distractions and desires, recognizing that they hinder spiritual progress. By withdrawing the senses from external objects and turning the focus inward, individuals can cultivate deep concentration and inner absorption.

Krishna teaches that meditation is a gradual process that requires patience and consistency. He emphasizes that one should approach meditation with sincerity, devotion, and a tranquil mind. By regular practice and detachment from worldly attachments, individuals can gradually attain a state of profound meditation and spiritual awakening.

Moreover, Krishna discusses the concept of the "self within the self." He explains that the true self, the eternal soul, is distinct from the physical body and the mind. By directing one's awareness to the inner self, individuals can transcend the limitations of the body and mind and experience their divine essence.

Krishna reveals the ultimate goal of meditation, which is the realization of the self and attaining union with the universal consciousness. He explains that through meditation, individuals can experience the divine presence within and recognize their oneness with the entire creation.

"The Yoga of Meditation" chapter serves as a guide for individuals seeking to deepen their spiritual practice through meditation. It offers insights into the techniques and principles of meditation, emphasizing the importance of solitude, discipline, and detachment. By practicing meditation with sincerity and perseverance, individuals can transcend the limitations of the mind, experience inner peace, and realize their true nature as divine beings.

◆ ◆ ◆

Title: Danny and the Secret Garden

Once upon a time, in a peaceful village, there lived a young boy named Danny. He was full of energy and loved to explore the world around him. But Danny had a little problem; he often found it hard to follow discipline and rules.

One day, while playing in the village square, Danny overheard some of the older kids talking about a secret garden hidden deep in the forest. They said that it was a magical place, where the flowers danced and the trees whispered stories to those who could find it.

Curiosity sparked within Danny, and he knew he had to discover this mysterious garden for himself. The older kids warned him about the dangers of wandering into the forest alone and urged him to wait until he was older and wiser. But Danny's excitement clouded his judgment, and he decided to venture into the forest that very afternoon.

Bewildered Danny enters the magical garden

As Danny entered the forest, he felt a rush of excitement. The tall trees seemed to reach out to him, and the sound of rustling leaves filled the air with a sense of enchantment. However, as he ventured deeper into the woods, he realized he had lost his way.

Panic set in, and Danny's heart raced. He couldn't find his way back, and the forest grew darker as the sun began to set. Fear gripped him, and he wished he had listened to the older kids and followed their advice.

In the distance, Danny saw a soft glow, like fireflies dancing in the dusk. As he moved closer, he discovered a warm, golden light illuminating a beautiful garden. It was the secret garden the older kids had spoken about! But instead of feeling joyful, Danny felt guilty for disobeying and putting himself in danger.

Just then, a wise old gardener stepped out from behind the flowers. "Ah, young one," he said gently, "I see you have found the secret garden. It is a place of wonder and magic, but it is also a place where discipline is essential."

Danny hung his head in shame, realizing his mistake. The gardener continued, "In this garden, everything thrives because of discipline. The flowers bloom when they are watered regularly, and the trees stand tall because they are rooted firmly in the ground. Discipline helps us grow and become better versions of ourselves."

Danny listened intently, understanding the importance of discipline more than ever. He felt remorseful for not following the rules and guidelines set by others who knew better.

The wise gardener smiled kindly at Danny and said,

"You are still young, my boy, and it is natural to make mistakes. The key is to learn from them and remember the value of discipline in everything you do."

With a newfound sense of understanding, Danny promised the gardener that he would strive to be more disciplined from that day forward. He thanked the gardener for his wisdom and guidance and headed back to the village with a heart full of determination.

From that day on, Danny changed his ways. He followed the rules set by his parents, teachers, and elders. He realized that discipline was not a restriction, but a path to success and happiness. He became a better student, a helpful friend, and a responsible member of his community.

As the years passed, Danny grew into a wise and disciplined young man. He often visited the secret garden, not just to admire its beauty but also to remind himself of the valuable lesson he had learned that day.

And so, the story of Danny and the secret garden spread throughout the village, teaching everyone about the importance of following discipline and how it could lead to a life filled with wonder, growth, and magic.

CHAPTER 7: THE DIVINE QUALITIES

Krishna enlightens Arjuna about the nature of divine and demonic qualities, guiding him towards a life rooted in righteousness and spiritual growth.

Krishna begins by describing the divine qualities that lead to spiritual evolution and inner fulfillment. He highlights virtues such as fearlessness, purity of heart, self-control, and a steadfast commitment to truth. These divine qualities contribute to one's spiritual progress, harmony in relationships, and the well-being of society as a whole.

Krishna explains that those possessing divine qualities are free from negative tendencies such as anger, greed, and jealousy. They exhibit humility, patience, and forgiveness, fostering a compassionate and inclusive mindset. Individuals with divine qualities act with integrity, treating all beings with respect and kindness.

In contrast, Krishna explains the characteristics of demonic qualities. Those driven by ego, selfish desires, and delusion exhibit qualities such as arrogance, deceitfulness, and an insatiable thirst for power and material possessions. Such individuals harm themselves and others, contributing to discord and suffering in society.

Krishna warns Arjuna about the consequences of succumbing to demonic qualities, emphasizing that they lead to spiritual ignorance and bondage. He urges Arjuna to cultivate divine qualities and rise above the destructive tendencies of the ego, as they obstruct one's spiritual growth and inner peace.

Furthermore, Krishna emphasizes that the divine qualities arise from a purified and self-disciplined mind. He encourages Arjuna to practice self-control, moderation, and the cultivation of virtues to develop these divine qualities within himself.

Arjun satisfied with all the knowledge
that Shri Krishna imparted

Krishna explains that individuals can choose their paths and shape their characters through their thoughts, choices, and actions. By consciously nurturing divine qualities and restraining demonic tendencies, one can transcend their limitations and strive towards spiritual excellence.

The chapter serves as a guide for individuals

to reflect upon their own qualities and behaviors, encouraging self-assessment and personal growth. It teaches the importance of cultivating divine qualities as a means to attain spiritual liberation, inner peace, and harmonious coexistence with others.

Krishna reminds Arjuna that those who embody divine qualities experience divine blessings and guidance in their lives. They progress on the path of spiritual evolution, ultimately attaining union with the divine consciousness.

"The Divine Qualities" chapter serves as a reminder that one's character is shaped by their thoughts, intentions, and actions. It highlights the significance of cultivating virtues and overcoming negative tendencies, leading to a more fulfilling and spiritually aligned life. By embodying divine qualities, individuals can contribute to the well-being of society and foster an environment of love, harmony, and righteousness.

❖ ❖ ❖

Title: The Kindness Castle

In a faraway kingdom, there stood a magnificent castle at the top of a hill. But this was no ordinary castle; it was known as the Kindness Castle. It was said that the castle itself was magical and could sense the goodness in people's hearts.

In the nearby village, there lived a young girl named Misha. Misha was known for her compassionate nature and willingness to help anyone in need. One day, as she was wandering through the woods, she came across a lost and frightened baby deer. Without hesitation, Misha gently picked up the little creature and took it back to her home. She cared for the deer and made sure it was safe until its mother could be found.

Word of Misha's kind act reached the ears of the wise old king who lived in the Kindness Castle. Intrigued by the young girl's goodness, he invited Misha to the castle to meet him. Misha was both nervous and excited to meet the king, but she knew that her heart was pure, and she had nothing to fear.

As Misha entered the grand castle gates, she felt a warm and welcoming energy enveloping her. The walls seemed to glow with a soft light, and the air was filled with a sense of love and harmony. The wise old king greeted Misha with a warm smile, and she felt an instant connection with him.

"Dear Misha," said the king, "I have invited you here because I sense the goodness in your heart.

The Kindness Castle can only be seen and entered by those whose hearts are pure and filled with kindness."

Misha taking care of the baby deer

Misha was amazed and humbled by the revelation. The king continued, "In this castle, we celebrate and honor acts of goodness and kindness. Those who live here understand that true happiness lies in being good at heart and showing compassion to others."

Misha nodded, feeling grateful for the opportunity to be in such a magical place. The king showed her around the castle, and she met the castle's residents – kind-hearted beings from all walks of life who had been drawn to the castle by their goodness.

As Misha spent time in the Kindness Castle, she learned valuable lessons about empathy, forgiveness, and selflessness. She saw how acts of kindness, no matter how small, could have a ripple effect, touching the lives of many.

One day, while exploring the castle's gardens, Misha met a sad and lonely little girl named Emily. Emily had lost her family and had nowhere to go. Misha's heart went out to her, and she decided to befriend and care for Emily.

As the days passed, Misha and Emily became the best of friends. Misha introduced Emily to the Kindness Castle, and together they learned the true meaning of being good at heart. They helped others, shared their joy, and spread kindness wherever they went.

The wise old king observed Misha and Emily's friendship and was pleased to see how they embraced the values of the Kindness Castle. He knew that their goodness would continue to grow and shine, making the world a better place.

And so, Misha and Emily lived happily in the Kindness Castle, surrounded by the warmth of love and the magic of their good hearts. They knew that the truest treasure in life was not gold or riches but the goodness they carried within them and shared with others.

And from that day forward, the legend of the Kindness Castle spread far and wide, inspiring children and adults alike to be good at heart and make the world a kinder, happier place for all.

ABOUT THE AUTHOR

Dr Arushi Mishra

Dr Arushi Mishra is a dentist and a public health professional. She loves to read and travel. Apart from her job, she is also a founder of a start-up with a vision to provide a platform for artists, creative personalities, and others to monetise their content in various geographies. She firmly believes that in today's entrepreneur world, we need such examples where women lead a change by initiating actions and organisations that are more social.

Being from a traditional Hindu family, she has always been interested in ancient Hindu texts. She feels that kids would relate more to the learnings of scriptures if it is told in the form of a story. She aims to write a set of books that would help the children know our religion and understand the deeper meaning hidden in these texts.